Poetry Of The Heart

By Deborah M. LaMot

@Copyright 2002

Publisher's Cataloging-in-Publication
(Provided by Quality Books, Inc.)

LaMot, Deborah
  Poetry of the heart / Deborah M. LaMot - - 1st ed.
  p. cm.
  LCCN 2002090526
  ISBN 0-9718200-7-4

  I. Title.

PS3612.A5466P64 2002   811'.6
                          QB102-701318

Cover Design by Olivia Roumie / Kimberleigh Graphics, Inc., N.Y.
Interior Design by Publishing Professionals, New Port Richey, FL

Manufactured in the United States

Visit our Website at:
www.PNDAJPublications.com

Dedication

In memory of my beloved sister, and best friend, Denise, who has always been my rock. You gave me the strength and courage to do anything in life I put my mind to. You were always there in the middle of the night when I needed someone to talk to. You will always be in my heart and I know you are watching over me. I did it buddy, and I have you to thank for it. I will always have you in my heart forever. I dedicate my book to you. Rest in peace in the arms of our Lord, and I will see you soon. I love you.

Table of Contents

Acknowledgments

I want to thank my Mom for the support she has given me through the years. She has made me the strong, independent woman that I am today. She always had faith in me, even when I didn't have faith in myself. Thank you for putting your life on hold so that you could raise your six children and teach us right from wrong. Thank you for always being there when I needed a shoulder to cry on, and for always understanding without criticizing. I love you more than words can say.

About the Author

Deborah is the youngest of six children and has been writing poetry since the age of 18. She is now 38 years old, single with no children. Worked as an agent for a freight company for 15 years. Her first poem, "The Beginning Of Life," was written the day she first experienced death, up close and personal. She went to her first funeral for a very close friend's father who passed away. She realized then that she was given a gift from God, to put words on paper of all the emotions she felt in the form of poetry. After her first poem was written, she then started writing poems when ever she was going through an obstacle in her life. Whether it was happy, funny or even her times of disparity, writing was the only way she knew how to deal with her feelings. After writing each poem, she would read it to herself and a healing process would take place. It was as if someone was giving her words of compassion, strength, and faith to pull her through her trials. It was a way out, a place to hide for a while. She listened to the heartaches of people around her and realized that she was not the only person trying to cope with life. This is why she wrote her book. If just one person can be touched by her words, it would be worth everything in life. God has blessed her, and through her poetry, he will bless you. Her favorite quote is, "With God all things are possible," Mathew 19:26, and so they are. She is living proof.

Together Forever

Many years of carrying your burden,
Always giving all you've got,
Never revealing you were in pain,
Never knowing when to stop.
You pushed and never once stepped back,
When others tried knocking you down,
Your courage, strength, and understanding,
Was like no others to be found.
If I can be anything like you,
I'd start with your big heart,
You gave even when you didn't have,
Which I was blessed to be a part.
You taught me the meaning of life,
How to cope and deal with a world so cruel,
I've learned from you to be myself,
And to be nobody's fool.
It seems like just yesterday I had you here,
I miss you everyday, every minute,
I'll carry you in my soul forever,
This world is lost without you in it.
I need to live a happy life,
Because that's what you'd want of me,
I no longer fear my last day on earth,
For together we will once again be. . . .

This is for you Buddy

A Clone Of Love

I remember back, when I was a child,
A middle class family, was my lifestyle,
Christmas was a happy time for us,
Leaving cookies and milk for Santa, was a must.
I have three sisters and two brothers,
A family of eight, with my mother and father,
We had a lot of times that were bad,
There were also happier moments we all had.
My father was never home, always at work,
My mother stayed home, to watch us and cook,
We never went without one meal,
With schoolwork and cleaning, my mom had to deal.
If I knew then, what I know now,
I'd ask my mom, to take a bow,
Times were hard, and yet she survived,
For her children, she made better lives.
Always hiding behind this big wall,
I always looked up to her, as she stood tall,
Being both parents, it wasn't easy,
She'd cook, clean, watch over us, as she kept busy.
I'm the youngest, the baby of the family,
Now being older, I can look back and see,
Watching all of us make our mistakes,
While she sat back, with her heartbreak.
She knew there was nothing she could do,
We would learn from them, this she knew,
To this day, she's there for us all,
When we have problems, when we'd take a fall,
I hope when I have a family of my own,
I'd be the mother she is, I'd be her clone. . . .

A Family

I'd like to settle down one day,
As I get older, I'm more set in my way,
It's harder for me to adapt to another,
I try my best, then say, "why bother?"
Why can't I find someone who's tamed,
Who's not lazy and doesn't complain,
Who can cook and help with the cleaning,
Not assume it's my job, and stop leaning.
I'm tired of being taken for a ride,
Feeling abused and hearing the lies,
I look at my life and something is missing,
I want to talk and for once have them listen,
Am I expecting too much out of life?
Is it asking too much to be a wife?
I guess if its God's will, it'll be,
The day I can say I have a family. . .

A Mothers Love

From the day we came out,
Of our precious mothers womb,
We felt the tender love,
Like a night with a full moon.
Just the sound of her voice,
The songs of her cries,
She rocks and cradles us,
With her sweet lullabies.
To watch us grow older,
Realizing she had to let us go,
When we reached the point of maturity,
Still allowing her love to flow.
Because of her, we're much wiser,
With the knowledge she gave,
Always watching and protecting us,
As she tried guiding our way.
I think the hardest job,
Are being both mother and friend,
When you have that relationship,
It's a gift that's God sent. . . .

A New Beginning

The ways of life are hard sometimes,
We reach a point, we're in a bind,
But when we cross that unknown path,
We need to find a way to latch.
Hold on to the good times then,
Where memories are kept, our hearts amend,
There are times you think of the bad,
Just put behind all that is sad.
Bring forth your light, and let it shine,
Be yourself, and don't fall behind.
With this in mind, follow your dream,
Whatever it is, your soul will be clean.
Of all the hurt, that once was there,
Your confidence and courage will let you bare,
The low you once felt before,
You'll look back and close the door.
We all have needs, which someday will come true,
If we have the faith to start anew,
We all have it in us, to bring it out,
To go on with life, without a doubt.
The moral to this poem, is to let it go,
New seeds in us, we'll have to grow. . . .

A Perfect Picture

All my life I've been overweight,
Always trying my best to fit in,
Trying different ways to lose the weight,
When do I start? Where do I begin?
Each day of my life, being criticized,
A world of hell waiting to explode,
My mind spinning, my heart racing,
How do I lift this heavy load?
I promise myself, I'll start tomorrow,
A day which never comes my way,
I stress myself, and eat some more,
Always making excuses for delay.
With magazines exploiting women,
To look like a perfect picture,
They snip, they tuck, and they plaster their faces,
Not one of them are pure.
No wonder why we torture ourselves,
To look like something not of this earth,
Everyone trying to please other eyes,
It is what's inside, that is your worth.
When you can love yourself for who you are,
You can start living life free of care,
Stop worrying about what others think,
And mend your heart of tears. . . .

A Question Of Love

I have thoughts in my mind,
About this man that I know,
I have feelings for him,
But I can't let them show.
Because of the doubts,
And fear of rejection,
I'm afraid to let go,
And show my affection.
Does he like me as a friend?
Does he like me the way I hope?
These questions go through my mind,
Then I think it's all a joke.
I'm tired of pretending,
These feelings aren't there,
But who am I really kidding,
It's just that I am scared.
I want to tell him,
How much he doesn't know,
Of all my feelings for him,
But my heart keeps saying no.
I don't want to get hurt,
If I can avoid it, I will,
But there's always a chance,
Until my dreams are fulfilled.
I know how it feels,
To be a puppet on strings,
To be pulled and yanked,
And to believe anything.
It's getting to the point,
I say, "I can't let myself fall,"
"In love with this man,"
And say, "to hell with it all.". . .

A Rainbow With A Voice

What thoughts go through your head?
When you see a rainbow in the sky?
Do you wonder how the colors form?
Do you ask yourself, why?
When colors appear before your eyes,
As if they were right there,
Each color having a meaning,
When you stop to stare.
Imagine each of these layers,
Being a part of our life on earth,
Each color having a time and place,
The first color means your birth.
As you look from top to bottom,
You notice the color change,
From the darkest to the lightest,
You think to yourself, "how strange?"
If we had the power in us,
To make our own rainbows,
What colors would we pick?
Would any of us even know?
We have the choice to do it,
To find our colors within,
If we had the faith to build one,
Our work on earth would begin.
Each of us having a spot,
To line up in the sky,
When our Lord comes back for us,
We can kiss the earth good-bye.
I know He has a place for me,
He gives us each the choice,
When we all can love our Lord,
We'll have a rainbow with a voice. . . .

Be Yourself

There are times when you want,
To be like the others,
When you feel left out,
A person no one bothers.
When most of the times,
They look at you strange,
When you're not like them,
You feel you have to change.
You want to fit in,
And be like the rest,
Make a few friends,
Not knowing what's best.
You have to realize,
That most of them are wrong,
When they do the bad things,
It makes them feel strong.
So who cares about them,
And what they think of you,
Just be yourself,
In whatever you do.
Do what is right,
You'll have no regrets,
When you see the others fall,
On that you can bet. . . .

Beside You

I've looked so far,
To see the light,
I've ran like lions,
Yet still the fright.
There's something missing,
Inside my soul,
My heart feeling empty,
My body is feeling cold.
As rain drops freeze,
On the coldest days,
Like ice sickles on an edge,
I wait for sunrays.
As I start to feel warm,
I finally feel proud,
Then the rain comes in,
And the sky becomes a cloud.
I don't know how to feel,
My body goes numb,
My mind racing fast,
As my head is hung.
I've got to give up,
And stop fighting my fate,
I need to humble myself,
Before it's too late.
There'll be days of sun,
Everyday will be new,
So when the clouds come in,
The Lord will be beside you. . . .

Best Of Friends

Two little girls, out in the park,
One always feeling used,
The other, never knowing what's wrong,
One friendship being abused.
She tries reaching through her,
And feels there's just no hope,
The youngest is the weakest,
Again she just can't cope.
It's too much to handle,
She wants to be best friends,
Again, there's the youngest,
Who feels hurt never ends.
The younger of these two,
Has always felt misplaced,
The other being stronger,
With freckles on her face.
There are years of good memories,
A lot of times they got mad,
But through it all they stayed,
As love they always had.
Now they're so much older,
These two are now adults,
They now are both women,
Filled out and all grown-up.
Through all these years,
There's been some pain,
There's been a lot of closeness,
And that still has remained.
These two little girls,
The youngest, felt weren't friends,
Are now part of each other,
The closest they've ever been. . . .

Beyond Emotions

Sometimes I feel I can't go on,
Why am I still around?
I analyze and criticize,
And yet I still feel down.
I try my best to make things right,
Keeping busy all the time,
While doing that, pushing away,
The real feelings in my mind.
How do I cope with this?
What is it that I feel?
Who is really suffering here?
As I think this can't be real.
I don't know what to do,
Or how I should react,
To all the needles and the tests,
What is fiction? What is fact?
I know my family loves me,
With that I have no doubt,
But how do I explain to them?
I just want the best way out.
I need to learn how to deal,
With what will be in store,
I have to put my trust in God,
To fix what has been torn. . . .

Birds Of Paradise

I look out my window at the sky,
I hear the birds singing their lullaby,
The sound of their voices, sounds of their song,
I know with you, is where I belong.
You bring me light, when I see dark,
Our love is solid as a rock,
My love for you means everything,
The symbol of this, is our ring.
I wear it with hope and with pride,
Without you darling, I know I would die,
My life with you, means more to me,
Than life itself, you hold the key.
To my heart and to my life,
I'm so glad we're husband and wife,
You brought to me a precious child,
For both of you, I'd walk the mile.
There will be roads ahead, with twists and turns,
But we'll do it together, our marriage is firm,
So when you feel down, and think it's all gone,
Please read this poem, and know we belong.
Together for life, no matter what's ahead,
Remember our vows, the day that we wed,
Don't ever feel alone, always think twice,
You and I will always be, birds of paradise. . . .

Can We Work This Out?

Can we talk without screaming?
Can we hold hands like we use to?
Can we just snuggle by the fire?
Can we make the old become new?
I want to work this out.
We got married for better or worse,
We're not richer or poorer,
When we met, we were each other's first.
We've been down this road before,
Always finding our way back,
Why can't we pull together?
And put our marriage back on track.
Let's try going out more often,
To a movie or out to dinner,
Spending more time listening to each other,
Let us come back again as winners. . . .

Co-Workers From Hell

Everyday is a challenge for me,
I wake up, get dressed, then leave,
To go to a job that doesn't care,
Always feeling I'm being deceived.
Anxious to get all the work done,
My mind racing as my heart pounds,
Doing five things at one time,
While everyone else is sitting around.
They order their food, discuss their lives,
Meanwhile the phones are ringing off the hook,
"Let her get it" they all are thinking,
As I pick up the phone like a jerk.
When will I be appreciated?
When are they going to wake up?
When will they care if the job is done?
As they stand there, filling their coffee cups.
Sometimes I really think it's just me,
Maybe I shouldn't be the way I am,
I should just be like the rest of them,
Sit back and not give a damn. . . .

Customer Service

Each day that goes by,
When night falls, I need to sigh,
What a day from hell,
So many stories to tell.
The customers are never satisfied,
I feel like my hands are tied,
I can never make them happy,
Everything they want done, snappy.
Lord give me patience to deal,
With the headaches and anger I feel,
The problems I have are my own,
I can't handle these stupid phones.
The anger is within me,
I can't find a way to set it free,
Taking it out on everyone else,
Bringing stress home with myself.
I need to trust in you my Lord,
To have patience you've already bore,
You will guide me your way,
I'll just take it day by day. . . .

Divorce

Mommy sat us down one day,
Told us Daddy had to go away,
Things don't work out as we plan,
It's hard for children to understand.
What can they say to explain?
That we the children aren't to blame,
They know the love we have for them,
How do they help our hearts to mend?
We must believe they will always care,
We know they love us, far or near,
It's hard sometimes when feeling down,
To find our father not around.
We see him on visits once a week,
The memories we have, we'll always keep,
Whether they're together or apart,
They'll always love us with all their heart.
I thank God I have their love,
Not seeing them together, is sometimes rough,
But when I need a guiding hand,
They will join together and take their stand. . . .

I still have nightmares of that morning,
It was cool outside and the rain was pouring,
I thought I was fine, and felt so secure,
Behind the wheel as my engine roared.
The roads were clear, no cars around,
If only I could forget that crashing sound,
I remember waking up, facing the wall,
I looked at my friend, as her name I called.
"Are you all right? Just stay still,"
I was fine, as my eyes filled,
With feelings of fright, and of guilt,
I tried to be calm, as my tears built.
The rescue team was there in a flash,
We both got in ambulances, as they dashed,
I walked out of the hospital, my nerves a wreck,
My friend stayed behind, with a broken neck.
The guilt I felt, nothing could compare,
I just kept saying, "it's just not fair,"
She later recovered, months down the road,
Living a healthy life, as I carry the load.
One night of fun, is not worth a life,
Just thinking about it, cuts like a knife,
So if you ever thought, "it's no big deal,"
Just think twice, before getting behind the wheel.
I thank God we both are alive,
The Lord saved us, "don't drink and drive." . . .

Don't Ever Quit

Thoughts of fear entered my head,
It scared me so much, I wished I were dead,
I'd think of situations I couldn't get out of,
Then I'd look up, to the heavens above.
I felt so guilty, I couldn't pray,
I'd put off my prayers until the next day,
The days came and went, and so on and on,
Once again, my prayers were never done.
Away from the truth, away from reality,
I knew I was wrong, just didn't want to see,
I blocked out the world, and kept to myself,
When my family was there,
I'd put them on a shelf.
I put behind all of my hurt,
Kept it inside, as I felt like dirt,
If only I let my Lord intervene,
I would have been strong, I would have felt clean.
Don't ever let pride stand in your way,
Humble yourself and be not afraid,
Our Lord watches over us, with his arms apart,
Waiting for us to open our heart.
We need to have faith in God's precious son,
When we all are together, the battle is won,
Until that day, my Lord carries me,
I see his footsteps, I am now free. . . .

Drugs Aren't The Answer

Days of depressions, angers and fear,
Went on in my life, as I wiped all my tears.
I wish I like myself, the way that I should,
I felt like killing myself, I wished that I could.
When I was twelve, I remember when I smoked,
It made me feel cool, the first puff made me choke.
Smoking led to drinking and got worse through the years,
I wished I never started, but I thought no one cared.
A few years later, I then started dealing,
I used it myself, it gave me a good feeling.
It took me away, from the real world outside,
Away from reality, a place to go hide.
I was hooked very hard, on every drug ever made,
Until I met someone, who took that all away.
It all started one night, when I was sleeping in my bed,
I felt this weird feeling, as if I was dead.
I saw a dove flying, with its wings spread out wide,
It got closer to me, and sat by me side.
It looked up at me, as if giving a sign,
To get up and walk, and follow behind.
It led me to a door, and behind it was bright,
I could see it seep through, like a thousand-watt light.
I reached to open it, and saw there wasn't a knob,
It was on the other side, trying to open it was a job.
I knew behind it, there was a place that was nice,
Far from what we live in, a land of paradise.
Then the dove was gone, I woke up from my dream,
I didn't think I was sleeping, it was real, so it seemed.
I knew there was a message, there is a better place,
I'd have to change my ways, if I want to live in His grace.
I then went to my dresser, pulled my draw out, then sobbed,
All my drugs were missing, and what was left was a knob. . . .

Faith

I feel so lost, where am I now?
There's no one here, not a soul around,
The walls are dark, where's the light?
As I fight back with all my might.
I can't see, where is the door?
I want to see light, as I had before,
How can I possibly get out of here?
I can't take the pain, I feel the fear.
Someone is here, but I cannot see,
I hear a voice, as I fall to my knee,
"Take my hand, I'll set you free,"
"From all your fears, just believe in me." . . .

Family Support

I have the whole world in my hands,
With a loving family who understands,
When I make mistakes or do something wrong,
I always have their love to carry me on.
To push myself to the best of my ability,
Never lets me give up, and put their faith in me,
When I need a shoulder or someone to lean on,
They help mend my wounds and show me I'm strong.
I couldn't imagine what it would be like
Not to have their advice to tell me what's right,
They criticize without giving any blame,
Make the clouds disappear and takes away the rain.
Whenever I feel lost, with no where to go,
Always working by butt off, with nothing to show,
I know I could always count on their support,
To pull me back up from the battle I just fought. . . .

Fate

When I'm with you,
My life is complete,
The world's easier to handle,
My problems I can defeat.
Without you in my life,
My world would fall apart,
I feel even when you're not with me,
You're in my soul and my heart.
I feel with you, like I've never before,
With anyone I've ever met,
We're just starting our new life together,
And there's going to be more yet.
We have so many things in common,
As if we were always meant to be,
I believe in fate, that our lives are planned,
That's how I feel with you and me. . . .

Flight 93

As they boarded the plane that morning,
Little did they know, hi-jackers they were storing,
These evil men thought for their God they would die,
To destroy innocent lives as we ask ourselves why?
Our loved ones did not die without a fight,
They took over that plane with all their might,
To save thousands of people they never met,
Knowing they'd die, they did it with no regret.
Because of the love they had for their country,
They didn't allow another disaster to be,
Now in the arms of our Almighty God,
We are left behind to bare the scars.
They now are at peace and eternally free,
We will never forget our heroes on Flight 93. . . .

Forbidden Love

I knew a man that once was so kind,
I'd think about him all of the time,
He had this overwhelming control over me,
Without any thought of his own family.
He knew how to impress, he knew what to do,
He took me under his wing, and I flew,
I felt like I was flying on cloud nine,
If only I knew, it was all just a line.
I thought he loved me, I knew I loved him,
I sacrificed my life, I committed a sin,
My life with Jesus was all torn apart,
I knew it was wrong, I didn't open my heart.
To hear the words my Lord had in-store,
I closed him out, I slammed the door,
It was my first love, I was so nieve,
The fact he was married, I couldn't conceive.
I put my Lord, which meant the most,
On the back burner, so that I could boast,
Boast about what? I had no idea,
This man never loved me, he didn't even care.
I now know the love, I thought I had found,
Was the kind of love that should be bound,
Any man who could go astray,
Can't ever be trusted, in anyway.
They say we learn by our own mistakes,
A better life for me, my Lord will make. . . .

Forgiveness

A long time, I did wait,
Until it was to late,
To say what I needed,
A new soul to be seeded.
I tried crying for help,
To myself, with it, I dealt,
Had no where to turn,
Kept it all inside, until my stomach churned.
I got to the mental state,
That only death was my fate,
This guilt is not worth,
Making me feel like dirt.
The one thing that held me back,
I could hurt her, that was a fact,
When I spoke with my friend,
The two years of torment was at end.
To bring my mind at peace,
And have my soul released,
She took the news well,
As my guilt, I did tell.
Now I worry about her,
With the friction I stirred,
I never wanted her hurt,
For my mistake it wasn't worth.
I almost lost my life,
Then hurt a friend, his wife,
A lesson well learned,
Don't play with fire, you'll burn.
Never to lie again, I choose,
I'll live with it, will be my dues,
Cope with life, the best I can,
Thank the Lord, she forgave me my sin. . . .

Free Your Soul

Don't take for granted all you have,
Take every moment as if it's your last,
Don't put off today, what you can do tomorrow,
Life is to short and goes to fast.
Take a moment to enjoy the view,
While driving down the streets,
Smell the flowers, listen to the birds,
Enjoy the company of people you meet.
We're only here on a visitor's pass,
Each having a different expiration date,
There will be a day when your visit is up,
You won't have to worry about being late.
So the next time you stress yourself out,
About what to wear or if you'll be on time,
Worrying about who will say what,
It really won't matter, you'll leave it all behind.
Just live your lives with a pure heart,
Filled with love, kindness and honesty,
Be good to others and build your faith,
If you do this, your soul will be free. . . .

Friends For Life

All the years of growing up,
All the toys we had,
We broke them, worn them, even shared,
And yet we still got mad.
I at you, and you at me,
We never seemed to stop,
But somehow, someway, along the line,
We always came out on top.
All the fighting, all the bickering,
Was worth it all these years,
Just to know that we are friends,
And how each other cares.
For one another, and for life,
And what our friendship means,
We know each other inside out,
Like a book it seems.
In the future there will be,
More friends to see and meet,
Some will stay and some will go,
But I'll be here for keeps,
When you need a pair of ears,
Or shoulder to lean on,
Always know that I am here,
For you to call upon.
What I'm really saying is,
We really need each other,
Those years mean a lot to us,
A friend there is no other.
You're a young lady now,
With your own life to lead,
Get a husband, have a child,
These utensils you'll need.
God bless you and your future,
And whatever lies ahead,
I love you kid, I'll never stop,
Remember these words I just said. . . .

Game Show Jitters

Did you ever watch those silly game shows?
Vanna White under letters, her stupid little pose?
The outfits she wears, just makes me sick,
Her little skinny butt, I'd just like to kick.
Or the one that give answers and questions you guess?
We're screwed up enough, we don't know east from west,
And the one where we guess, whose telling the truth,
Who really cares, I think they're all a bunch of kooks.
How about the one that play notes to a song?
Contestants sing and look like asses when they're wrong,
The one with Barker, what's that about?
With no dye in his hair, it finally comes out.
One day he has brown, the next day he has white,
I can't tell you the feeling of fright,
And what's the purpose of Family Feud?
The title alone, adds fire to the fuel.
And we wonder where people get crazy ideas,
Do they wake up one morning and say, "Let's Make A Deal?"
People steal from stores, and what they take they keep,
I know what they're thinking, "hey, Supermarket Sweep!"
It's like life's not passing fast enough,
They have to have game shows like Beat The Clock?
We have gamblers, who think their problems are mild,
That's because they're all home watching Jokers Wild.
We have congressmen always passing the buck,
What do they think this is? Press Your Luck?
What is next? When will it all stop?
When we're all at home watching Shop Till You Drop? . . .

Godson

I look into his eyes,
And wonder what he thinks,
So precious is this little one,
With his perfect lips so pink.
What does he see before him?
As he looks into my eyes,
Does he know who I am?
As I sing him a lullaby.
A part of this child's life,
I feel so blessed to be,
I'll do my best to teach him,
What has been instilled in me.
Can't wait to see him grow,
As I cherish all the fun,
Seeing him grow into a man,
To be proud to call Godson. . . .

Goodbye

It's Christmas Eve and all is quiet,
Alone in my room I sit,
While memories of you run through my mind,
As the clock on the wall ticks.
I remember all the times we shared,
We shopped, wrapped gifts, we laughed all night,
Guessing what we got for each other,
I never did guess it right.
This holiday was your happiest time,
As we opened all your gifts,
You'd be so excited to see our faces,
As our spirits you would lift.
I wish I had you here with me,
Never thought I'd live without you,
I feel so lost and empty,
I just don't know what to do.
You always wanted the best for me,
For you I'll lift my head up high,
And walk the path that God has given,
I'll see you soon my friend, goodbye. . . .

He Has A Purpose

I know the Lord has a purpose for me,
He gave Moses the power to part the seas,
With Abraham, He gave twelve nations,
I keep the faith, to have the patience.
There will be a day, when the Lord will reveal,
What is my purpose? What is his will?
I feel the power to touch other lives,
With my poetry, I could change a life.
If this is his will, I know I'll succeed,
With my testimonies, his children I'll feed,
The Lord is no longer on that cross,
All the pictures of him, we can all toss.
It's the symbol of the cross, without him on it,
That will bring to mind, his power and spirit,
He bore the sins of every man,
So we could have power, to take over this land.
Without him in your life, this earth isn't yours,
We all have a purpose, He knows what's in-store,
Just kneel down, as you bow your head,
Humble yourself, and your spirit will be fed.
Listen to his words, and know his love,
He knows what we can bare, He knows what's enough,
He'll guide you every step of the way,
For our transgressions, He has already paid. . . .

Heartless

I'm always complaining about my life,
Walking around with a puss on my face,
Everything I see and everything I hear,
I seem to always feel out of place.
I look for all the negative things,
Never giving any chance for the positive,
Always bringing down the spirits of others,
Not taking advice from others who give.
I do what I want, who cares who I hurt,
As long as I'm not on the receiving end,
You can say whatever you want about me,
I can care less about who I offend.
If this sounds cruel or somewhat heartless,
Because I love to be the bearer of bad news,
Then take a good hard look in the mirror,
This poems not about me, it's about you. . . .

He'll Protect You

Which is better, happiness or sin?
A battle of loss or win?
Which would you prefer, if given the choice?
To listen to Satan? or the Lords voice?
Do you walk across a highway? Or a road?
Would you carry a feather? Or a load?
Would you walk through a fire? Or swim in a pool?
Go through life smart? Or being a fool?
There are many trials we need to bare,
The Lord did it all to show He cared,
No one is perfect, we all make mistakes,
We need to reach out, our hands He'll take.
He'll pick you up, dust off your feet,
Stand by His side, the devil you'll defeat,
Life's full of changes, which way do we go?
Keep your faith strong, let His seeds grow.
We've got so many things to decide,
It's just much easier with the Lord by your side,
He'll love and guide you as much as you allow,
We need to commit, to take a vow.
Believe the Lord, is your Savior,
Let Him in your heart, He will save you,
Know His words and know He's true,
No matter what's ahead, He'll protect you. . . .

I Spend My last Days

When the morning is here,
And everything is bright,
I look out my window,
And see the beauty in the light.
Because I know soon,
I won't get the chance,
To sit back in my chair,
And watch the birds dance.
To see all the colors,
Of the leaves in the fall,
To hear all the birds sing,
When their mothers call.
To see the time,
For them all to move on,
To make room for more,
Once their young are gone.
To watch the squirrels,
Gather their nuts,
To prepare for winter,
In their little made huts.
Others' don't appreciate,
The world which we live in,
Till the time they have to leave,
Then they want to begin.
By then there's no time,
To enjoy beauty in everything,
I'm glad I had the chance,
To see what happiness it brings.
I'm not afraid anymore,
Just getting close to the end,
I know I'm going to meet Him,
Face-to-face, my friend.
I won't have to worry,
About how it feels to die,
I will soon see that rainbow,
When I breath my last sigh. . . .

35

I Wish

I wish yesterday didn't pass,
I wish the good times would always last,
I wish you were here with me,
I wish together we could always be.
I wish I didn't say good-bye,
I wish I cried my last cry,
I wish I could stop feeling cold,
I wish your hand, I could hold.
I wish I could give you a kiss,
I wish you being here, I didn't miss,
I wish my faith were a little stronger,
I wish my hurt, I felt no longer.
I wish I knew how to feel,
I wish you leaving weren't so real,
I wish I knew when the Lord would be back,
I wish His knowledge I didn't lack,
I wish I could go home with you,
I wish all the above would happen soon. . . .

If Only We Were Doves

You and I are as of doves,
Flying in the sky,
I know if you weren't here for me,
I would surely die.
My life with you means more to me,
Than life itself my love,
So glide with me in the air,
To reach the heavens above.
We can search for our new lives,
Where ever it may be,
It doesn't matter where it is,
As long as you're with me.
It's as if when we're together,
The sky and clouds depart,
And the sun shines on our faces,
And shows what's in our hearts.
When the sun goes down,
And darkness fills the air,
I know I need not worry,
For you are always near.
Between us a rare relationship,
A lot in common too,
That's why we're so good together,
Each day with us is new.
If we had the choice to be,
Anything in life,
I'd like to be a dove, who's free,
In other words, your wife.
So we can fly far away,
To go with the wind and sky,
Do whatever our hearts desire,
And kiss the ground good-bye.
Everyday my love grows stronger,
For you it never ends,
So stay the way you are for me,
And always be my friend. . . .

911 In God We Trust

There was not one cloud in the sky,
To work we went as we kissed our loved ones good-bye,
Not knowing what will soon come our way,
Would change our lives forever and will never be the same.
When the first plane struck we all thought was error,
Then came the second, we were all in terror,
The sky that was clear has now turned black,
Our innocence taken away we can never turn back.
We will be strong and become as one,
As America will do what has to be done,
Our hearts go out to the families of this disaster,
We can't stop the cries, where there once was laughter.
We will not go down without a fight,
America will bond together and will unite,
For the heartless cowards who thought they'd destroy us,
We are stronger than ever for IN GOD WE TRUST. . . .

It's Not Religion

Christ has died, Christ has risen,
Christ will come again,
It's all I heard, in my life,
Until I became born again.
When belief is titled, such as religion,
Everything's a routine,
You kneel, you pray, you don't even speak,
His word not heard or seen.
Nothing is gained, by going on Sunday,
And being a part,
Unless there's love, and the spirit of Christ,
Inside your own heart.
The Word of God, is all I need,
To get me through the day,
It's not religion, it's not tradition,
It is the only way.
Most people try, to get what I have,
And still they don't succeed,
You need His word, you need His spirit,
You need Jesus indeed.
If someone tells you, your way is strange,
And doesn't stay your friend,
Just take the trials, like Jesus did,
He's with you till the end. . . .

It's Time

It's time to cast our anger away,
It's time for us all to pray,
It's time to feel each other as one,
It's time for us to prepare for God's Son.
It's time for you to look into my eyes,
It's time we stop hearing our cries,
It's time to put your hatred aside,
It's time for us all to just abide.
It's time for us to put our Lord first,
It's time for us to stop the curse,
It's time we listen to the Father,
It's time to love our sisters & brothers. . . .

Jesus The Light

There's a twinkle, a glow,
That people seem to see,
Something that is life,
A part they need to be.
They want what I've got,
But just can't find it,
If only they knew,
It's free, you can't buy it.
The light that is shown,
Is a spiritual glow,
That shines on my face,
To let the world know.
To show there's a peace,
An everlasting love,
That only one can give,
And comes from above.
So I'll let it shine,
So everyone can see,
What Jesus Christ my Lord,
Has made of me. . . .

Judgement Day

Hear about the man that cheated on his wife?
She walked in and caught them in the act,
I tell you if that was my husband,
I'd take everything from him, and that's a fact.
How about the man that came out of the closet?
I would have never guessed, he hid it so well,
It's amazing how people can live in a lie,
I know he is definitely going to hell.
I can't believe that women who killed her children,
How could a mother ever think of doing that?
She's a sick individual and should be executed,
They should beat her to death with a bat.
It is so easy for us all to judge people,
Who are we to think we have the final say?
We will each be convicted of our own sins,
A sentence which will be announced on Judgement Day. . . .

Just Be Silent

I need some time to myself,
Without you breathing down my neck
I need to just take a moment,
When my nerves are just a wreck.
Step back and give me space,
When you know I have things on my mind,
I don't need your opinions,
Just turnaround don't look behind.
Not every problem you can solve,
Until the day you walk in these shoes,
You could never know how I'm feeling,
Always preaching your don'ts and do's.
You think you have all the answers,
When in fact you haven't a clue,
Always saying, "just let it go"
Telling me what "you" would do.
Just be silent for awhile,
Sometimes I just need to shed my tears,
Just hold me as close to you as possible,
Then my emotions I can share. . . .

Just Imagine

Imagine a field of blooming flowers,
The grass so perfect, and behind it a sunset,
The sky is filled with colors of orange,
The dew on the flowers that make them wet.
While walking through it, the feeling of freedom,
Imagine if you can, this place afar,
As you look around, you see nothing but beauty,
You feel so peaceful, with the gleaming stars.
You can shout loud, and hear your echo,
The sounds of birds singing their praise,
Hearing the voices of all life's creatures,
No cars, no horns, you feel in a daze.
We take for granted all these things,
That God has created for us to enjoy,
Imagine what would happen if we realize,
The Lord has better for us in store.
Imagine the ground as moist and soft,
For the grass and flowers to have a way to live,
How can this be happening? What is the answer?
All this, and more, our Lord will give.
Why ask how? Or where this comes from?
There's only one answer, we need the faith,
To know who's behind it, who has this power,
It is His will, which is our fate.
We have all this, if we live His way,
He gave His life, to forgive us our sins,
If He could create this lovely field,
Heaven is better if we just imagine. . . .

Let Down Your Guard

We're always the one to be pushed aside,
When all we're doing, is trying to abide,
In His laws and the laws of the land,
It's hard for people to fully understand.
When we show our concern and our caring,
If only they knew, it's His love we're sharing,
When will we know? When will we learn?
When we're all in hell, waiting to burn?
Satan is a liar, the Bible will tell,
We need to get out of his wicked spell,
Have faith in the truth, and in our Lord,
You'll find His words will cut like a sword.
All we have to live on, is our faith,
We can build mountains, that's all it takes,
God is alive in each one of us,
We were all created from ashes and dust.
If you have any doubts, just look around,
At the skies, the trees, and the ground,
If we're wrong and there's no Lord,
We have nothing to lose, nothing in-store.
What's wrong with living a healthy life?
Having faith and finding we're right?
We'll never know, until our final day,
That's where faith comes in, believing anyway.
Not knowing for sure, but believing in our hearts,
Just put your trust in Him, and He'll never depart,
Life will go on, far after we're gone,
But we'll always have that special bond.
I'd rather live life, without being behind bars,
Have faith in His words and let down your guard. . . .

Life Support

All she wanted to do,
Was to ride around,
With the new bike that she got,
Then she was tossed to the ground.
The driver didn't see her,
Until it was to late,
He was coming down the street,
At a very fast rate.
The ambulance drove up,
And took my baby away,
To the hospital down the street,
As I looked where she lay.
She means more to me,
Than anything in the world,
She's only ten years old,
She's my little baby girl.
They took her in a room,
Ripped off the clothes she wore,
I was told to wait outside,
As the nurse closed the door.
The doctor told me to sit down,
As he talked calm to me,
He told me she was staying,
She's on a life support machine.
"This can't be happening,"
I remember saying,
"It's all just a dream,"
As I see her laying.
Everyday I pray to God,
I know the Lords there,
I'm not giving up on her,
Because I know Christ cares.
He keeps me going,
I know where He stands,
He never lets me down,

My baby's in His hands.
Eight months have gone by,
She's still asleep in her bed,
Doubts of my faith,
Keep running through my head.
I walked down the hall,
As I do everyday,
To be by her side,
And I'm never away.
I hear a voice in the room,
As if she knows I'm coming,
I throw my purse on the floor,
And then I start running.
I opened the door,
And there I could see,
My baby girl sitting up,
As she calls out for me. . . .

Love Never Dies

Someone once told me,
If a love was real strong,
A rare flower would grow,
To each other they'd belong.
I once had two dogs,
Their breed was Labrador,
I fed and loved them,
I couldn't ask for more.
I named one Bonnie,
The other I named Clyde,
Both took to each other,
And were always by my side.
Everyday I'd wake up,
As early as I can,
I would take the dogs out,
And watched as they ran.
One day I went outside,
Then looked all around,
Where they usually played,
But my dogs weren't found.
Clyde showed up later,
Bonnie was left back,
He grabbed my hand,
As I followed his tracks.
I saw Bonnie laying,
She was hit by a car,
I could see the blood,
Eventhough I was far.
A few hours passed,
When I buried my friend,
The relationship we had,
I thought would never end.
Months went by,
Clyde got weaker everyday,
He hadn't eaten much,
Since Bonnie's been away.

He missed her so much,
I could see his sad eyes,
Every time I looked at him,
It just made me cry.
Then one day came,
When I found Clyde dead,
I remember the tears pouring,
As I lifted up his head.
I went to the place,
Where I put Clydes love,
Next to Bonnie I buried him,
Then looked up above.
Weeks then went by,
Before I could go,
To the ground they laid,
Because my feelings were low.
I walked towards the graves,
And tears fell from my eyes,
Between them grew this flower,
Their love never died. . . .

Marines Home Coming

It seems like a lifetime,
That we've awaited his coming,
It's finally going to happen,
There won't be anymore running.
He's been away for so long,
We won't know what to say,
When we meet him at the station,
On the evening of this day.
We have so many thoughts,
Of reminiscing the past,
It has been awhile now,
And it hasn't gone fast.
The time is getting closer,
Our family will soon be together,
We will finally see our baby,
Just like he wrote in his letter.
We regret him every signing,
The papers to be a marine,
But he served our country well,
We're just grateful he can leave.
We can see his train now,
It's on the way down the track,
The anticipation is building,
As we hold our tears back.
We see someone, who looks like him,
It can't possibly be,
For his face is of an older man,
Could it be him that we see?
The train comes to a stop,
We can't see him anywhere,
Crowds of people gather around,
There's a voice that we hear.
We turn around and there he was,
With opened arms and tears,
He hugs and gives us both a kiss,
With his uniform he wears.
"It's so lonely without you,"
"Many dreams of you I've had,"
"I'll never leave you again,"
"I love you Mom and Dad." . . .

50

Marriage

A sacred vow between two,
That binds together with love,
Nothing can come between it,
A match made from above.
Sometimes there'll be problems,
And you'll think you were wrong,
In the commitment you've made,
But you have to be strong.
Love is everlasting,
And can conquer anything,
It makes a marriage work,
The symbol is the ring.
Faith in each other,
And showing that you care,
When support is needed,
And always being there.
When a vow is made,
It's not only to each other,
It's coming from the heart,
Showing your love to the Father.
When you say, "I do"
These two words are the key,
Of sharing two lives,
And starting a family.
When the sun goes down,
Then you begin your new life,
When you realize the next day,
That you're husband and wife.
Learning each others ways,
And talk everything out,
If this isn't done,
Then there'll always be doubt.
Treasure the moments,
Through your whole life,
You both are as one,
You're husband and wife. . . .

Misled

Don't think because you get flowers,
Or maybe some affection,
You have someone who will be there,
When you need support and attention.
You start putting your life aside,
And start living for another,
Carry all their burdens and problems,
Because you now have a lover.
Who you think one day will be,
The future of all your dreams,
The love you've waited all your life,
When your eyes light up and gleam.
My advice to you, I can only say,
Don't disregard the flags that are red,
Take it slow and don't jump the gun,
Keep this in mind, you won't be misled. . . .

My Knight

There I was, in a place afar,
Somewhere out there, is my shining star,
I wait to see that shooting light,
When I look up, with the stars so bright.
One night there'll be, up in the sky,
One star gleaming, as it shoots by,
It'll be bright as sunshine on pure white snow,
Like a field of flowers, with one red rose.
I looked down the road, as far as I can,
The road got narrow, as I ran,
I stopped to look at what I could see,
I then realized, what is meant will be.
I need to praise him and not think about tomorrow,
In His path I need to follow,
It'll be when I'm ready, He'll be there.
When the time is right,
The Lord will open to me that door,
Behind it will be, my knight. . . .

My Little Angel

There's a life breathing inside of me,
My dream has come true to start my family,
Can't wait to see my baby's eyes,
Will they look like his or look like mine?
The time is near for our bodies to part,
No longer will two, share the beat of my heart,
The bond I feel could never be explained,
With what I will have, will be worth this pain,
My baby is here, my life is complete,
As I look down at his tiny little feet.
There will be so many stories, to him I will tell,
First will be the day God sent
My little angel. . . .

My Noel

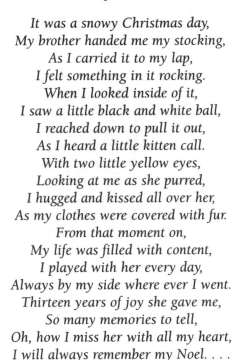

It was a snowy Christmas day,
My brother handed me my stocking,
As I carried it to my lap,
I felt something in it rocking.
When I looked inside of it,
I saw a little black and white ball,
I reached down to pull it out,
As I heard a little kitten call.
With two little yellow eyes,
Looking at me as she purred,
I hugged and kissed all over her,
As my clothes were covered with fur.
From that moment on,
My life was filled with content,
I played with her every day,
Always by my side where ever I went.
Thirteen years of joy she gave me,
So many memories to tell,
Oh, how I miss her with all my heart,
I will always remember my Noel. . . .

My Savior

There were times in my life,
I felt there was nothing to live for,
Then He came unto me,
With the robe that He wore.
As a light in the dark,
Shining down on my face,
He said, "be not afraid,"
"For you are at His grace."
"Have faith in Me,"
"And follow my path,"
"Know I died for you,"
"To save you from His wrath."
If you believe in His power,
And that He died for you,
Believe in His words,
Then there's nothing you can't do.
Know He's always with you,
And know His revelations,
He will never leave or forsake us,
Through our trials and tribulations.
Just confess with your mouth,
That Jesus Christ is Lord,
Always remember the Father,
And who He was crucified for.
Though He's not here in the flesh,
He will leave us never,
In our hearts and our spirits,
He is with us forever.
We must await His coming,
When He feels the moments right,
We will not know when,
He'll come as a thief in the night.
When the time is here,
The moment we must capture,
For when we see Him,
It'll be the day of rapture.

When His children are gathered,
In one place and accord,
We'll look into His eyes,
And know He's our Lord. . . .

New Year Resolution

My goal for me will be this year,
I'll put behind me all my fear,
To look ahead with a new attitude,
Not be so negative and stop being so rude.
No more complaining about what's not done,
I'll wake up everyday and cherish the sun,
Every breath I'll take as if it's my last,
Follow God's will and do His task.
This world is just a resting-place,
To teach me what I need to face,
I'll learn of life and how to be kind,
Put all my bitterness and hatred behind.
Treat the world, as I'd like to be,
Treasure every moment with my family
If I can do this, then I'll be set,
To live this year with no regret. . . .

Next Stop Heaven

Three years have come and gone,
Not much in my life is new,
Still in the same place I was then,
My friends are now very few.
I can't get past that dreadful day,
My life still feels torn apart,
God please guide me through this pain,
Help heal my broken heart.
Sometimes I feel my faith's not strong,
To help me deal with my loss,
What I would give to have the peace,
It won't matter how much the cost.
You're always there when I fall down,
Picking me up time and time again,
I know we must past this level on earth,
Next stop heaven, our wounds you will mend. . . .

No Longer Alone

I have this anger inside of me,
How do I release it, to set it free?
It sits on my shoulders like a heavy weight,
I'm getting anxious, as I anticipate.
So many ways I tried releasing the load,
When I think it's gone, another rocky road,
I see it coming towards me at a fast speed,
Trying everything in life to fill that need.
I can't find myself, don't know where to go,
I'm climbing this mountain, and there's nothing below,
It's getting so much harder, for me to climb,
I feel like giving up, and leaving it behind.
I can't give up now, it's at arms reach,
Like waves washing up, on a white sandy beach,
I see the water coming, as it pushes the sand,
It surrounds my feet, in the place I stand.
I allow this water to flow all over me,
With a feeling of warmth and tranquility,
I need not look further, for what's always been there,
I see the light shining, as angels I hear.
The battle is over, I can now go home,
Don't cry loved ones, I am no longer alone. . . .

No Right Or Wrong

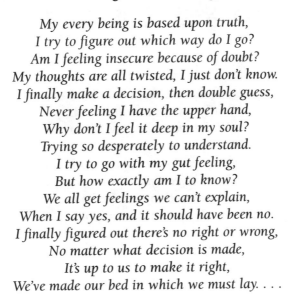

My every being is based upon truth,
I try to figure out which way do I go?
Am I feeling insecure because of doubt?
My thoughts are all twisted, I just don't know.
I finally make a decision, then double guess,
Never feeling I have the upper hand,
Why don't I feel it deep in my soul?
Trying so desperately to understand.
I try to go with my gut feeling,
But how exactly am I to know?
We all get feelings we can't explain,
When I say yes, and it should have been no.
I finally figured out there's no right or wrong,
No matter what decision is made,
It's up to us to make it right,
We've made our bed in which we must lay. . . .

One Of A Kind

There's a house far away,
That only few can see,
A place to start a life,
And have a family.
It has a housemaid,
With lots of beautiful rooms,
With thousands of windows,
To look at the views.
There are flowers in the garden,
There's streets paved with gold,
There's nothing but sunlight,
With no place for the cold.
When you look in the yard,
If you're one of the few,
You can see the gardener,
As He watches over you.
He trims the grass,
He waters the flowers,
He makes it a nice place,
As He works for hours.
He nurses his children,
He gives them love,
He protects and cherishes,
As He works from above.
When you need to go out,
His door will always be opened,
But to see this gardener,
You must confess what you've sinned.
Believe in His words,
Believe with all your heart,
Know He's there for you,
Then He'll be able to start.
To prepare his table,
For His family to be,
All together at once,
As He holds the key.

To the place full of beauty,
We can't imagine in our minds,
By faith I will live there,
Our Lord is one of a kind. . . .

One Wish

There's not one thing I regret,
As my life goes up and down,
Filled with tragedy and laughter,
While trying to keep my feet on the ground.
To see all life has to offer me,
Without asking for to much,
I'll try to be the best I can,
And not get caught up in the rush.
There's just one thing I would change,
And it wouldn't be that I was rich,
To have you in my arms again,
That would be my one wish. . . .

Our Heroes

Without giving a thought of putting themselves in danger,
They dash up the steps to save a stranger,
As the heat and smoke surrounds their masks,
Knowing each step they take might be their last.
Their goal always being to save as many lives,
To bring them all home to their husbands and wives,
As they ran up the stairs while others ran down,
They had to keep looking until everyone was found.
America won't allow you to die in vain,
As our memories of you will always remain,
You're now beautiful angels with golden halos,
We love you all and you will always be our heroes. . . .

Panic Disorder

Do you ever go to the movie theatre,
When the loud noise surrounds you?
You take a deep breath to calm down,
It doesn't help whatever you do.
Or when you're in a supermarket,
As your standing on a line?
You feel like your being surrounded,
Feels like you're being rushed for time.
You think if you count to ten,
It will all have passed,
This feeling of desperation,
As you start breathing very fast.
This is a physical illness,
Not many people can relate,
Don't care what others think,
As you feel you're locked behind a gate.
Don't think you're going crazy,
Don't think you're the only one,
Who has this chemical imbalance,
When you feel you're all alone.
Anyone you pass on the streets,
You would never know by whom you see,
For we all hide it within ourselves,
We need to talk to set us free. . . .

Promises He Will Keep

Life goes on, so they say,
A saying I never wanted to hear,
How do I go on with my life,
Knowing you are no longer here.
Sometimes I feel like screaming,
I feel like punching the walls,
I think it's just a bad dream,
As I sit and wait for your call.
There has to be something I can do,
To change the hands of time,
If only I can bring you back,
And put my life in rewind.
I miss you my special friend,
Always know I'll be all right,
The Lord will watch and guide me,
He'll turn my darkness into light.
I know there's always a reason,
Why God has our fate planned,
We just have to trust in Him,
And put our life in His hands.
My faith is what keeps me going,
And knowing you're at peace,
Knowing God has you in His arms,
And all his promises He will keep. . . .

Psychiatric Ward

I feel so isolated from the world,
As if the clothes I wore were soiled,
I see people, who are in pain,
A learning experience, I definitely gained.
I look back to what was then,
Suddenly I realize, it's not the end,
There's a life out there, which I know is for me,
A new life, I know I could see.
This place is only a landing post,
To help the problems I feared the most,
After seeing what others have been through,
I know now, there's nothing I can't do.
I'll walk out, with my head held high,
Set forth my new beginning, with a sigh,
A sigh of relief, a sigh of hope,
It's a hard task, but I'll have to cope.
If life was simple, or just a breeze,
We would all be so very pleased,
Unfortunately we need to cross roads,
That could sometimes be a load.
We need to go to the point of no return,
In that way, we could prevent the burn,
I'll go forward, and won't look back,
I know now, I'm on the right track. . . .

Selfish

I always thought together for life,
Till the day you had to go away,
I've seen others go through the pain,
Just never thought it would come my way.
The day I received the phone call,
Was the last day of my life,
My heart felt empty, my body was cold,
As if I were being stabbed with a knife.
Not one day or hour goes by,
Memories of you and the love we shared,
Goes through my mind and in my dreams,
As this pain is so hard to bare.
I don't know how to stop this feeling,
I know my life must still go on,
But without you here, by my side,
I feel lost and all alone.
Knowing you're happier than you've ever been,
Surrounded with love, I could only wish,
The most beautiful sight you've ever seen,
Wanting you back would be selfish. . . .

Sexual Harassment

When a pat on the back,
Gets lower as time goes on,
When words are suggested,
When you feel something is wrong.
"He's my boss, a professional"
You think to yourself, "it can't be"
Trained to protect, to get the job done,
"There's no way he would do that to me."
"So he gave me a little kiss on the cheek?"
"It was a jester for the holiday"
Eventhough this happened last year,
And this year was on no special day.
Instead of rubbing my shoulders,
As he did a few times a week,
He now rubs down the front of my neck,
Standing behind me as he peaks.
"It's not happening, just all in my head"
"I'm taking this all out on content"
He brushes his hands through my hair,
"It's not like that, it's not what he meant."
It wasn't until that day, no one was around,
He walked up behind me, as I smelled his scent,
And put his hands down my blouse,
I realized then, it was sexual harassment. . . .

Smoking

All it takes is the first try,
You get hooked without knowing it,
Your body starts to crave more each day,
As you put one out, another is lit.
Not realizing you're now on two packs,
It is all we start thinking about,
As we run outside to take a puff,
And panic when our last pack is out.
We've tried so many times to quit,
Always ending up smoking more,
Waking up in the middle of the night,
Just to make a trip to the store.
It's not our life we should care about,
It is our loved ones, who are watching us die,
When they're left behind to bare the pain,
To live without us, and ask themselves why? . . .

Soap Opera Mania

As I drive home in my car,
I can't wait to rewind my VCR,
Each day I make sure the timer is set,
To tape my soaps, on that you can bet.
All day thoughts go through my head,
As I wonder who came back from the dead,
Each day never knowing what to expect,
Which couple is divorcing? Who died in a wreck?
Who over heard a phone conversation?
Who crashed a wedding, without an invitation?
What were they thinking, when creating these shows?
Were they preparing us for life, as only they know?
If we really think about it, it's kind of sick,
We depend on soaps, just for the kicks,
When we get home, we get rid of our men,
So we can sit back and watch, "All my children."
Are Tadd and Dixie really getting married?
Who died suddenly and is now being buried?
So desperate to watch them, anything we'd give,
Just as long as we taped, "One life to live."
Who was behind killing Victor Lord?
Will Dorian get Vicki, to settle the score?
What will happen on, "General hospital?"
As Luke and Laura unbury a skull.
A body that's been dead for 20 years,
Give me a break! Who really cares?
I guess we care, and will never learn,
As we get caught up in, "As the world turns." . . .

Soccer

Run, run, run, and get to the goal,
Kick, roll, swerve from side to side,
Get past your opponent anyway you can,
Cross your legs and take a dive.
I don't care how you play,
As long as I see you are trying,
I don't want to see pushing and shoving,
And definitely none of your whining.
Do the best you can when you play,
I only want to see your devotion,
In this game we call soccer,
There is no time for emotion.
Don't take this game to heart,
Shouldn't matter if you lost or won,
What matters is if you enjoy yourself,
Just get out there and have some fun. . . .

Something A Child Can't Be Taught

A child has a dream,
That one-day they'll be grown,
With ambition and courage,
To make it on their own.
Until that child is older,
He will never understand,
In order to get what he wants,
He'll have to learn to take a stand.
With decisions and compromises,
And all life has in store,
He'll have worries and fears,
That were never felt before.
But through life's journeys,
He'll learn how to cope,
Something a child can't be taught,
All his parents have is hope.
Hope that he'll survive,
In this world full of pain,
To keep his moral values,
And keep himself sane. . . .

Starting Over

I'm leaving behind my old life,
Going away to start over again,
I hope I'm making the right choice,
But with what I now have, I will win.
A better life I'll try to have,
No longer will I keep myself inside,
For the fear of meeting the wrong people,
Always finding a place to hide.
I will now be able to open the blinds,
To let the light shine through my windows,
The room will no longer be dark,
As I set forth my new goals.
I have nothing to leave behind,
A lot more to live for,
Doing now, what should have been done,
Along time ago, when I shut the door. . . .

Still

Still waiting for that door to open,
Still waiting for your call,
Still waiting to hear your voice,
Still waiting for you down the hall.
Still wondering why you left me,
Still wondering what to do,
Still wondering how to feel,
Still wondering who to go to.
Still here when you're not,
Still living day by day,
Still having doubts of my faith,
Still not knowing, why you went away.
Still I know you're in a happier place,
Still I know you're free,
Still hard for me to handle,
Still trying to be the person you want me to be.
Still waiting for the day to come,
Still knowing we'll be together again,
Still keeping my faith in the Lord,
Still knowing you're no longer in pain. . . .

Thank You

Thank you for always being there,
Thank you for giving me strength through my despair,
Thank you for knowing me better than anyone else,
Thank you for helping me take care of myself.
Thank you for never turning your back,
Thank you for giving me knowledge I lacked,
Thank you for leading me through the trials,
Thank you for answering when I dialed.
Thank you for picking me up when I fall,
Thank you for coming to me when I call,
Thank you for giving me the strength I need,
Thank you for healing my wounds when they bleed.
Thank you for giving me only what I can bare,
Thank you for allowing me to shed my tears,
Thank you for mending my heart and have it restored,
Thank you for choosing me as your child, My Lord. . . .

That's Life

What is going on with you?
Why can't you talk to me?
I try to express my concern,
And all you can say is "let me be."
It hurts to see you in pain,
Not knowing how to help,
I want to wrap my arms around you,
Instead you sit by yourself.
You have this look on your face,
As if the world has just gone away,
Leaving you with no where to run,
As you sit in your room all day.
You're not the first to feel this way,
And you're certainly not the last,
We've all had our crosses to bare,
Life will teach you, to let it pass. . . .

The Beginning Of Life

You look in the sky,
And you wonder what's there?
When you look at the clouds,
And you stop to stare.
Is there something behind them?
Something we can't see?
Maybe a place of happiness?
But, "no it can't be."
Is it possible for us,
To believe such a place?
Where there's beauty and peace,
And a glow on our face?
Our minds play tricks,
And confuses our soul,
When we finally start believing,
Our body takes hold.
It tells us these lies,
And makes us believe,
That there's no such place,
As we all are deceived.
Where there's no feeling of hate,
Angers or fears,
No feeling of hurt,
No meaning of tears.
If only we knew,
The world thereafter,
Where there's nothing but brightness,
And the sounds of laughter.
We seem to have thoughts,
Of our bodies being life,
And when it gives in,
It's the end of our lives.
This world is a level,
To which each have to pass,
In order to reach,
That threshold that's last.
When our bodies are dead,

And our hands are cold,
It's just the beginning,
Then our spirits take control.
It takes us away,
From the pain we bare,
Of this worlds' headaches,
And its worries and fears.
It's a place of warmth,
Filled with life and love,
That only one can give,
That's the Lord up above.
Next time you think,
These things can't be real,
Let Him in your life,
His touch you will feel.
So when we mourn the dead,
And think life's unkind,
It is them, who are crying,
For leaving us behind. . . .

The Bible

Words of encouragement,
Words of fear,
Words that show love,
Words with care.
When there are times you need,
A friend to talk to,
Just open it up,
And He'll talk to you.
Each word is alive,
And shows it when read,
You must have the faith,
So that your spirit is fed.
If you ever have a doubt,
That these words aren't real,
Just read a few pages,
His touch you will feel.
So remember when your down,
And climbing a steep hill,
Just read His words,
For that is His will. . . .

The Choice

Did you ever have one of those days?
When nothing goes right no matter what you do?
You try to make it better, and it gets worse,
When you get home, you just sit and stew.
There'll be brighter days, as you think ahead,
You say it'll get better next hour,
You wait till then, for it to happen,
And instead, the worst has power.
When I have this kind of day,
When nothing seems to be right,
I put away my bad moments,
And look towards the Lords light.
He lets it shine on every man,
Believe in our Lord and His love,
I know with Him, I'll get through the day,
He makes me feel, as if I'm a dove.
Flying in the sky, feeling so free,
Breathing in his air, as I fly,
Looking down at His land,
Kissing the ground good-bye.
Take each minute, one moment at a time,
Each day we have, is a gift from the Lord,
Think of Him every second of the day,
Build your faith and cut that cord.
Believe in Him, and know His word,
Pray each day, He hears our voice,
With our faith, we can live better lives,
He gave us the power, to make that choice. . . .

The Chosen

Through the miracles of life,
A child is born of thee,
Not knowing how special He is,
Or what His future will be.
Yet as He grows up learning,
He is not like any other child,
There is something about Him he feels,
That is not of anyone's style.
He has visions of what lies ahead,
As He matures into a man,
Strange things begin to appear,
As He tries to understand.
He hears a voice in the air,
"You have a lot of work to get done"
It was that day He realized,
He was chosen as Gods' son. . . .

The Graduate

It's all over and the grades are past,
Time to move on and do your task,
There's a life out there, I know you'll succeed,
With ambition and courage and self-esteem.
You can do anything you put your mind to,
Follow your dreams, this you can do,
Nothing comes easy, without the devotion,
Put your skills and your mind in forward motion.
You must always believe in yourself,
The child you once were, just put on a shelf,
You're an adult now, with a new attitude,
Be the best that you can, in whatever you do.
Put your foot forward, and don't look back,
With this in mind, you're on the right track. . . .

The Medication Of Christ

When we're sick, we go to a physician,
We trust in them to give us medication,
When we're tired, we shut our eyes,
As we sleep, our bodies energize.
When we're hungry, we know when to eat,
When we sweat, we know it's the heat,
Our brain lets us know what we need,
It's how we live, it's how we breathe.
When water falls from our eyes,
It's our body reacting, and allow us to cry,
It tells us we're happy or we're sad,
When our faces turn red, we know we're mad.
Our body is a unique instrument,
It tells us secrets, and gives us hints,
Of what to expect and how to feel,
Our brain circulating blood, like a wheel.
Flowing through each muscle and vein,
How can this be? Can anyone explain?
God created our body as His temple,
The body of Christ, it's that simple.
He's in total control, from head to toe,
He nurtures us, when we're feeling low,
Christ is our brain and we're the hearts,
His spirit is our blood, of our body, is a part.
If we let His spirit, like our blood, flow,
His spirit will feed us and let us grow,
Our bodies would die, without these three parts,
Trust in our Lord, we'll be shield from the darts.
Life is a gamble, like throwing the dice,
We need to take the medication of Christ. . . .

The Ocean

If you stop and listen you can hear a faint whisper,
The sound of the breeze calling out to you,
The sky field with colors of orange and yellow,
As you feel the crisp air of the morning dew.
You can look far across to the horizon,
Where there's a place of peaceful solitude,
As the sound of waves crash against the rocks,
You've forgotten the problems that have troubled you.
Feeling the soft sand beneath your feet,
While another day is getting ready to begin,
Well, I have to go back to the chaos of life,
But you can bet, I'll be back to see you again. . . .

The Power Within

The sun is shining, the sky is clear,
The birds are singing, their songs of cheer,
I have this feeling, I can't explain,
My soul is crying, please help my pain.
I look to the clouds, and give a smile,
It will all be over in just awhile,
Each step I take, I'm on my way,
I take each step, day by day.
To a place I know I've been before,
It's been so long, I can't remember anymore,
The way I was, the way I use to be,
When my heart was full and my spirit free.
Everyday I get one step closer,
My mind twisting and turning like a roller coaster,
I stop and think, there is a power,
Within me every second, every hour.
When I feel helpless as a child,
My Lord is carrying me every mile,
With His hand, on my shoulder,
His voice saying, "I will hold her."
Until I'm ready to walk alone,
He stands beside me, as I roam,
I'll be all right, my Lord is here,
He's watching over me, I will not fear.
I'll keep in mind, His love is true,
And begin my life, and start anew. . . .

The Puzzle

I'd like to think of me as kind,
Someone who you could depend on,
To help you go through life's downs,
Without saying whose right or wrong.
Sometimes I feel there's nothing to say,
Trying everything I can to help you,
What words can I say to express?
All the pain you're going through.
The best way I can explain,
To show you how to deal,
With the problems life throws at you,
To have your heart be healed.
Is simply let your emotions out,
Don't keep it all locked inside,
You need to release your tears,
Your feelings don't try to hide.
Don't try to be strong for everyone,
Picking them up when they fall,
Who will be there when you are down?
As ears lay deaf when you call.
Life's like a piece of a puzzle,
Which piece should go where,
To put what you have learned from life,
For others like you, to share. . . .

The Resurrection

All the miracles were shown,
And still not believed,
He gave them His love
And yet was deceived.
A man who preached words,
Which they didn't understand,
If only they would believe,
His hour wouldn't be at hand.
But to fill Gods scriptures,
This had to be done,
The world had sinned,
So He sent us His son.
He was later crucified,
With the sign, "King Of Jews"
Mary found the stone missing,
And told Peter the news.
The disciples went to the place,
Where His body was to be,
The clothes He wore,
Was all they could see.
When the third day came,
The disciples were in accord,
A figure stood in the midst,
And they knew it was their Lord.
"My father has given me,"
"The kingdom of glory,"
"I now give it to you,"
Now we don't have to worry.
We will sit with Him,
On the right hand side,
Of our glorious Father,
Our God the most high.
Jesus told His father,
"My work on earth is done,"
Satan thought He had victory,
But it was us that had won. . . .

The Stolen Car

I got off the train as I did everyday,
Went to the parking lot my car was in,
I walked over to where I left it,
My Nissan was gone, in my spot was a Lincoln.
I flipped out and called 911,
To let them know my car was taken,
If they think I'm not gonna put up a fight,
The police are in for a rude awakening.
I just bought this car five days ago,
They couldn't take the piece of junk I had before?
They waited for me to buy a new car,
I won't ever park in this lot anymore.
The officer called in my license plate,
I was asked to wait on the side
He came back to me laughing hysterically,
My car was in lot four, we were in five. . . .

The Time Will Come

Ever wonder what will happen,
When the end of time is here?
Will we all be ready for Him?
When our Lord Christ appears?
Like out of the blue, it will happen,
The sky and clouds will depart,
The sun will shine down from above,
Only He will know what's in our hearts.
It will be the day of rapture,
After that we'll all be judged,
Only one has the power to do this,
The one who died, to show us His love.
So why must we always gossip?
About everything and everyone?
We must learn to accept people,
For who they are not what they've done.
It's not for us to decide,
Who is right, or who is wrong,
We need to just worry about ourselves,
When we all do this, we'll be strong.
We need to love, which is sometimes hard,
To respect others, as you would them you,
Reach out and help, when given the chance,
Show our love, which is what we should do.
Life goes on, and we need the peace,
Our time on earth, is coming to an end,
But when we all come together,
The time will come, our Lord He'll send. . . .

The Wonders Of The Lord

When we see a flower grow,
And try to understand how?
When we hear a bee buzz,
When we drink milk from a cow.
When leaves from a tree,
Begin to fall down,
When light shines in the sky,
Before a loud thundering sound.
What is the reasoning?
How can we understand?
It is not for us to know,
But to follow His hand.
He'll guide and protect,
Till the end of our time,
When there's nothing left,
But our spirits and minds.
When we all meet Him,
Face to face at last,
He'll greet us with open arms,
When we're done with our task.
Don't think about tomorrow,
For it might never come,
Just follow the Lord,
He'll show us the sun.
He'll show us a place,
Our minds can't imagine,
When the time is right,
Then it will all begin.
When we all accept Jesus,
And we all are as one,
When we can love one another,
Then His work will be done. . . .

Then There Came You

I remember years ago,
In the back of my mind,
How I use to have no friends,
Even one who was kind.
Being kind to me,
Is what you have done,
Someone who is nice,
To be with and have fun.
I'm glad there is you,
Who I can always call,
Whenever I need someone,
When my fist is through the wall.
When my doubts are high,
And my feelings are low,
You're the one who understands,
A friend I'll never let go.
The one who would tell me,
When I'm right or wrong,
The one who'll be there,
Make me feel I belong.
At times I feel strange,
And just want to go hide,
Away from the world,
Away from their side.
Away from my troubles,
My worries and fears,
It's nice to know that you,
Are one who cares.
You mean a lot to me,
And that will never change,
The everlasting love I have,
No one will re-arrange.
All the woes, all the headaches,
You make them go away,
You give it to me straight,
Of what you have to say.

You bring me back to reality,
Then I know what to do,
I never had many friends,
Then there came you. . . .

There Once Was

There once was light, which was gone,
There once was peace and joy,
There once was a feeling of hopelessness,
There once was happiness, I ignored.
There once was a girl who never grew up,
There once was a life never fulfilled,
There once was a soul that was empty,
There once was a person without a will.
There once was a feeling that no longer is,
There once was a child never grown,
There once was that part of me,
There once was a person unknown.
There once was, is now in the past,
There once was, has a place to turn,
There once was, is no longer there,
There once was, I now have learned.
There once was that child, now older,
There once was sadness, I can say with a sigh,
There once was a girl, now a woman,
There once was, I can now say good-bye. . . .

Think Positive

When words are just to strong,
You need to keep inside,
The anger or the judgement,
Is best when left aside.
To sit back and look around,
See what you've got in life,
Enjoy all the beautiful moments,
And not cut it down with a knife.
The hardest thing for one to do,
Is let the heartache pass,
To take all your anger inside,
And let the good times last.
Forget the worst and the hate,
Let it go with the skies and wind,
You'll feel the burden lifted,
When that is done, you'll win.
You'll look at life different,
To see what has died, has lived,
To see life without the blind folders,
And not live your life so negative. . . .

This House

As we looked down the road at the horizon,
We saw this house we wish we lived in,
Just something about it, made us feel warm,
This house was beautiful, with a bright green lawn.
We imagined where our garden would be,
We'd plant tulips, and roses, with a few daisies,
We would finally have our own little yard,
Always living in apartments was always hard.
Our children never having enough room to play,
Always dreaming we would own a house one day,
When we saw this house, we knew it was ours,
It was calling our names as if it had power.
All we could think about was how good it would feel,
To finally walk through the doors, of a house that was real,
As we packed our last box, only God would have known,
We now live in this house, we could finally call our own. . . .

Unlock The Door

Where have you gone my little one?
Why haven't you called? Why did you run?
I'm here for you, whenever you need me,
Just call out my name, I have the key.
To open that door you feel trapped behind,
If only you open it, then you will find.
There's a way out, just let Him in,
Just turn the knob, He'll forgive you your sin.
The Lord is with you, He'll never let you go,
Until the end, allow His light to flow,
Through your spirit, He will fly,
Release your fears, and stop asking, why?
There's no need to feel ashamed,
He bared the cross, so that we could reign,
All His power, and all His love,
Will shine on you, like the sun above.
The clouds will clear from the skies,
We'll be free as His spirit flies,
Souring through all of our thunder,
Finding a way, so we need not wonder.
With all His power and His might,
He'll set forth, and make things right,
Have faith in Him, our time is due,
Our days are numbered, and oh so few. . . .

What Is A Sister?

Someone who cares,
When I'm out past dark,
Who's always there,
When I want to talk.
Who watches over me,
When I do things wrong,
Who guides me in the right path,
Who makes me feel strong.
"There's nothing you can't do"
She always tells me,
"Believe in yourself"
And I start to believe.
I see all the things,
I never saw before,
She gives me the confidence,
And she opens a door.
My goal is to be,
The best that I can,
In whatever I do,
And she tells me I am.
She's the one that I know,
Who'll tell me straight out,
How to forget all my worries,
And forget all my doubts.
There is something about,
Her unique way of living,
She shows me her love,
And she is always giving.
I'm glad I have,
A sister who cares,
The relationship we have,
Is very special and rare.
I love you sis,
As I know you love me,
My best friend in the world,
You will always be. . . .

When You're In Denial

When you feel the need you have to talk,
Then change your mind, and instead you walk,
Away from what you need to say,
You keep it bottled up and locked away.
You want to shout as loud as you can,
It gets to the point when it's out of hand,
You think you can handle it on your own,
You dial a number, then hang up the phone.
Where do you go? What can you do?
You're not alone, there's others like you,
You can't find a way to get it all out,
You try to analyze, what's this about?
Family and friends start to see you change,
You feel like you're losing it, you feel derange,
You have to realize, you can't do it alone,
You need the support, to let it go.
All the feelings of hurt and despair,
You're destroying yourself, it's to much to bare,
Release your feelings, don't hold them back,
You'll feel like a new person, that's a fact.
I know this, I was once in your shoes,
Take my advice, I promise you won't lose,
Your life's going to be filled with trials,
When you realize this, you're no longer in denial. . . .

Where Are My Keys?

I lost my car keys the other day,
Even looked in the freezer where my veggies lay,
Looked under my bed and on the TV,
Also in the bathroom as I took a pee.
Went upstairs to my closet doors,
Got on my knee's and checked the floors,
Back down the stairs to the living room,
I'm running late, it's already noon.
I should have been at work an hour ago,
What will I tell them? I don't know,
I'll look like a jerk if I tell the truth,
I guess I can fib, they won't have any proof.
Where are these keys? I'm getting upset,
I feel like kicking my beloved pet,
Walked past the mirror and saw something shine,
They were in my hand the whole time. . . .

Who Are You?

Who are you to tell me what's right?
Who are you to not let me fight?
Who are you to tell me where to go?
Who are you to say you know?
Who are you to judge my life?
Who are you to cut me down like a knife?
Who are you to think you know it all?
Who are you to think you're so tall?
Who are you to say anything you want?
Who are you with your words that taunt?
Who are you to think you can change me?
Who are you that you can't let me be?
Who are you to think you have the world?
Who are you always with me since a girl?
Who are you to follow my life so well?
Who are you all my mistakes you can tell?
Who are you that know everything?
Who are you that someone died and made you king?
Who are you, your words cut like a sword?
Who are you? I asked, "My child, I am your Lord." . . .

Your Hand I'll Hold

What are you doing to yourself?
Haven't I taught you well enough,
To know there's only one way to go,
When you go through times that are tough.
You never listen to what I say,
Always doing your own thing,
I try to warn you in advance,
And let you fly on your own wings.
I tell you what you need to know,
Trying to get through that thick skull,
On how to handle life's ups and downs,
Wondering why your hearts not full.
Time and time again, you never hear my words,
Shouting your name for you to come to me,
I see your face as you listen,
And yet you still just want to be.
I'll never give up on guiding you,
I love you with all my heart and soul,
Just know I'm always by your side,
As your Lord, your hand I'll hold. . . .

The way their little paws,
Grasps your hands,
As they get playful with you,
Yet they obey your commands.
They don't need any help,
In supporting their needs,
They defend themselves alone,
As they hunt for their feed.
What makes these little creatures,
So sweet and lovable?
You look into their eyes,
As they make you feel gullible.
They're so easy to talk to,
As you hold them in your arms,
Watch them play and run around,
As they throw around your yarn.
They don't need any training,
So independent and kind,
When you need their love,
They are beside you all the time.
With all the hair and fur balls,
And all their scratching,
You can't help but love them,
With all their running and catching.
They jump so high up,
When they see a flying bug,
It's so funny, you have to laugh,
As you give them a hug.
When you hear them purring,
You know they're satisfied,
I guess that's why they say,
That cats have 9 lives. . . .